BEHIND THE WINDOWS
OF A
SMILE

UNCOVERING THE HIDDEN TO WALK IN FREEDOM

BY TONYA KING

WTL INTERNATIONAL

Behind the Windows of a Smile

Copyright © 2021 Tonya King

Cover artwork by black_artt @ Fiverr

Published by
WTL International
930 North Park Drive
P.O. Box 33049
Brampton, Ontario
L6S 6A7 Canada
www.wtlipublishing.com

978-1-927865-91-0

Printed in the U.S.A.

I own my mess; it creates my message.
—Tonya King

Foreword

By receiving, giving and touching the lives of others, Tonya King has been expanding her capacity to reach those hurting in secret with concealed childhood and adulthood pain.

The effect of God's hand upon Tonya's life is evident; she is an impressive individual who cares about people. She demonstrates faith in Jesus the Christ, who is her problem solver.

This book lets you know that no matter what you are experiencing in this life, there is hope, and there is help. Despite Tonya's painful struggles and difficulties, she truly perseveres in trusting in the Almighty.

The God that she serves allowed her to experience illness, physical, emotional and psychological. She suffered the loss of loved ones, a failed marriage, the loss of career opportunities, and the list goes on. On the other hand, though, Tonya has experienced and enjoyed the presence of God; His hand is upon her life. Nothing that she has passed through and will pass through will be able to destroy her so long as she abides in Him. He promised never to forsake her on her life's journey.

I had the privilege to meet Tonya on June 7th, 2009. Over the years, she allowed me the opportunity to speak into her life and support her where needed. Our friendship is ongoing.

Tonya is qualified not through theory but her lived life experience. She acquired life lessons to pass onto her readers to enrich their lives to a greater level. Tonya permitted herself to be truthful and honest about the origin of her pain. She took it as a learning lesson and now chooses to use it as a teaching moment.

Be strong in weakness,

Be bold in adversity,

And when you have done all, stand, my friend and comrade in the common faith,

Keep taking a stand, singing, writing and sharing.

... so, Tonya's readers, read on and decide how you will face the challenges and handle the struggles in your life.

Pamela Anderson

Pastor, Teacher and Counselor

A Word from Pastor Ezekiel

Behind the Windows of a Smile by Tonya King is highly recommended for everyone. The author's writing style makes it easy for anyone to read. The simplicity, authenticity, audacity, and honesty she displays in sharing her personal experiences are quite intriguing. That can only have happened by the inspiration of the Holy Spirit.

I have known Tonya and her lovely family for many years. She is a very simple, lovely child of God who uses her life and talents to serve God and humanity.

When she passionately discussed this book's focus with me, the scripture that came first and foremost to my heart was about forgiveness. "And forgive us our sins, as we forgive those who sin against us. And don't let us yield to temptation" (Luke 11:4 NLT). Life is precious, and we must habitually forgive the people who have offended us and continually ask God to forgive and deliver us from all evil. For all have sinned.

The Good News is that all our sin-debts are paid in full. We are sanctified by the word of God and cleansed by the blood of the Lamb of God. We are reconciled and made at peace with God the Father by the Finished Work of Jesus Christ on the Cross. So, no matter the situation, God still loves us. I pray that your eyes of understanding will be opened, so you will see and affirm and declare God's love in your life.

As you read this book, let the testimonies shared encourage you to repent and believe in Jesus Christ. My prayer is also that this book will richly bless all its readers, bring honour to Jesus Christ and glorify God the Father. Amen.

Ezekiel Ezechim

Pastor

Grace Apostolic Ministries, Brampton, Ontario, Canada

Acknowledgements

First and foremost, I want to acknowledge, honour and give thanks to God my Father. He is the reason I am alive, and I dare to share my testimony with you today.

Secondly, I would like to thank my mom, Verdella, and my dad, the late Azariah King. They brought me up in fear of the Lord and encouraged me to reach for my dreams. I love you, Mom; you are simply the best. Thank you for being my greatest cheerleader.

I would also like to thank my daughter, Shilah. I love you so much, girl!!! Thank you for being patient with me and giving me the time to write this important book about my struggles with Childhood Sexual Abuse. Thank you for your love and support. I truly appreciate you for loving me unconditionally.

I would also like to thank and acknowledge the best sister-in-law in the world. Thank you, Shen, for being my personal editor and helping me organize my book while I had post-concussion challenges. I love and appreciate you.

I'd like to thank my nephews for trying to be quiet as I worked on this book. Thank you, my (younger, older) brother, Ceyion, for allowing your wife to assist me during the many days she did. I love and appreciate you.

I would love to acknowledge my entire family and extended family for their love, support, and prayers—you are all a true blessing to me. I thank God for a God-fearing network of family and friends.

I want to acknowledge my life coach, Dr. Hugh Anthony, who worked with me for two years of the twenty-plus-year journey it took to complete this book.

I must also acknowledge my psychologist S. Ault whose help has been invaluable.

I would like to also acknowledge my senior pastor, Pastor S.A. Morrison, Pastor Pamela Anderson, Pastor Janet Gordon, Pastors Ezekiel and Uche Ezechim, Pastor Frank Douglas, Pastor Marcus Martinez, Pastor Cassandra and Apostle Garfield Fray, Rev. Denise Gillard, Minister Elfreda Gordon, Minister Icyln Bowen, Evangelist Mary Bennett, and Dr. Sanneth Brown. Thank you all for your prayers and support in the areas where you contributed to my life. I will not forget where you have enhanced my spiritual journey with God.

Thank you, Farrah Hodgson, for the opportunity to become a co-author in my first two books; thank you for seeing and believing in me as a writer.

Thank you to all my friends and readers who have supported me along the journey by purchasing my previous books.

Thank you to all who believe in, encourage and support me as I pursue my purpose to live and serve for God faithfully.

Dedication

I dedicate this book to those who have gone through Childhood Sexual Abuse and are afraid to speak out because they have lost their voice—to those who feel like there is no way out and there is no hope for them to walk in freedom.

I also dedicate this book to my daughter, Shilah, to let her know that she can overcome anything!!!

Please remember! *You may be damaged, but you are not destroyed—* Tonya King.

Testimonials

Through reading Tonya's book and reading what she experienced, I learned many new terms and gained clarity on similar situations that I've been through myself. I also gained Godly insight and counsel on preventing myself from experiencing what Tonya went through and how to solve the situation should I ever end up in one again. Tonya writes and shares her testimony in a way that will have you glued to the pages, wondering what's going to happen next. I can relate to Tonya's experience and feel the emotions she pours into sharing her truth. Her chapter is spirit-led, and you can feel the authenticity and appreciate the vulnerability she displayed in sharing her story so that others can benefit.

—Rochelle Smith

Tonya always speaks from the heart. She always wants the best for those she communicates with. She won't gloss over the truth just to make it palatable to the reader. Tonya is a courageous young lady who will confront every circumstance with the truth of God's Word and persuade her listeners only to accept realities that are in line with God's best for them.

In her writing, Tonya displays a vulnerability that fully engages her readers: she draws us in and takes us on a journey where each scene is painted. Tonya describes her pain and joys, her losses and triumphs in a bid to urge us not to repeat her mistakes while pointing us to the best path of life found in Jesus' perfect will.

—Ima Ituen

Behind the Windows of a Smile looks into the life of a Childhood Sexual Abuse survivor. Coming from a raw and vulnerable place, the author pulls back the curtain on abuse to take you on a journey toward healing and freedom.

—Shenelle King

Writer, singer and dancer, Tonya is real. She lives what she speaks. She gives and keeps on giving. Tonya would be considered an old soul. She is connected to her environment and has a deep love for humanity. She spends time giving back to her community at home and abroad. Whether participating in her local community initiatives or her back-to-school charity events in Jamaica, Tonya is passionate about helping others.

In her chapter, *Pray, Don't Fall Prey,* in the multi-authored book, "The Process," Tonya opens up the cocoon of her life to share her vulnerability. However, it's the same as in the transformation process, where the once vulnerable and delicate larva emerges as a soaring butterfly. Like the beautiful, strong, and well-adored butterfly, there is no doubt in my mind that with her determination and many talents, Miss King will become known as the Monarch butterfly among her peers.

—Jennifer Williams

Table of Contents

Introduction

Behind the Windows of a Smile is the most extensive piece about myself I have ever allowed myself to write. I have always known that I was bound to write it and today is that day. I hid in the shadows of cold people in a cruel world for many years. I stood afraid with a smile on my face but filled with anger I could not express—hiding the rage with a smile.

This is a brief look into the story of my life. I call it a story because when I reflect on my life, it feels like I'm turning the pages of a storybook. In a story, the character starts happy, then sad, angry, frustrated, then tries to solve the mysteries of life and figure out what to do; then the answers come, and if the character makes the right choices, they live happily ever.

My life is no fairy tale, but I know that "…all things work together for good to those who love God, to those who are the called according to His purpose" (Romans 8:28 NKJV).

The purpose of this book is to help individuals who have experienced Childhood Sexual Abuse. To help them choose to become a victor instead of a victim. I want to let them know that they're not alone and help them find their voice.

I want to offer each reader some information to help you to understand Childhood Sexual Abuse better and help you develop the strength to own your experiences and choose to move from "pain to possibility," a phrase I learned from Dr. Hugh Anthony. I will do this by sharing with you my experiences and the things I did to move out from behind the windows of a smile.

1

I have included Bible passages to help to highlight important points. You'll notice abbreviations that follow quoted passages. Each of these abbreviations serves to communicate which translation of the Bible was used. NKJV stands for the New King James Version; NLT stands for New Living Translation; AMP stands for Amplified Bible, and KJV stands for King James Version.

What is Childhood Sexual Abuse?

Sexual abuse is any sexual contact between a child and an adult that uses the child for sexual purposes. It's most often done by someone the child knows and trusts. Sexual abuse does not have to involve penetration, force, pain or even physical touching. If an adult engages in any sexual behaviour with a child, including but not limited to looking, showing, or touching to meet the adult's interest or sexual needs, it is sexual abuse (Murray, *et al.*, 2014).

Sexual exploitation is another form of child sexual abuse. It happens when a child is talked into or forced into sex acts in exchange for things like money, food, drugs or shelter (Canadian Mental Health Association, 2013).

Usually, the perpetrator plans the incidents partly in order to feel power and control over another person (Government of Western Australia, Department of Health, 2021).

Why Talk About It?

Childhood Sexual Abuse (CSA) has been happening since the beginning of time. It occurs in society's shadows. No one is immune. Through my research for this book, I have found that it is a silent epidemic in all corners of the world. Take a moment to consider the following statistics:

- 1 in 3 girls and 1 in 4 boys experience an unwanted sexual act (Psychology Today, 2021a).
- 4 out of 5 incidents occur before the child is 18 (Educate 2 Empower, 2014).
- 20% of sexually abused children are under the age of 8 (Darkness to Light, 2015).
- The most vulnerable age to be exposed to CSA is between 3 and 8 (Educate 2 Empower, 2014).
- 95% of the victims know their perpetrator; only 5% of sustained child abuse offences involve a stranger (Educate 2 Empower, 2014).
- Children under 18 are at most risk of being sexually assaulted by someone they know.
- Older or more powerful children victimize up to 40% of sexually abused children.
- 70% of all adult perpetrators have between 1 and 9 victims.
- Sexually abused children are at a greater risk of mental health problems, suicide attempts and substance abuse (DefendInnocence.org, 2021).
- There is more lasting severe emotional damage when a child's sexual abuse starts before the age of 6 and continues for several years (American Counseling Association, 2021).
- Children who disclose their abuse within a month are at a reduced risk for depression (DefendInnocence.org, 2021).

Childhood Sexual Abuse is an urgent issue at all socio-economic levels and in all communities. CSA has caused many lives to be lived in confusion and has been fundamental to its victims' depressive tendencies and mental health challenges. The raging battles it leads to within victims' minds are a major stressor and can cause adverse physical health effects.

Behind the Windows of a Smile is for individuals who have experienced Childhood Sexual Abuse and are suffering silently. It's for families encountering challenges and issues as a result of sexual abuse within their family. It's also for people who know someone who has been through Childhood Sexual Abuse and want to let that person know they are not alone.

This book is not limited to those individuals, though: it is for anyone who has struggled with forgiveness.

I will provide insights, techniques, tools, strategies, ideas, and ways to recognize trauma and overcome it.

I hope that this book will give the voiceless a voice and courage so they can move from being a victim to become a victor.

I want to give each reader some basic knowledge to recognize the signs of Childhood Sexual Abuse and take steps to prevent it from happening within their own families.

My motivation in sharing this part of my life story is since I have gone through Childhood Sexual Abuse, I can help others by speaking out about it. It will help them effectively step out of their dark place where they may have felt alone in their trauma. They can then address it, recognize it and possibly escape the abuse by dealing with it appropriately.

Within this book, I speak my truth. I tell the truth about what happened to me based on my perceptions as a child, a youth growing up, and as an adult. I speak the truth about the effects experienced throughout my life. I talk about how I thought, coped, struggled, subsisted, fought, managed, and ultimately, survived until I began to thrive through resilience, perseverance, grace, love and God's forgiveness for myself and for those who took advantage of me.

1 Corinthians 6:18 (AMP)

Run away from sexual immorality
[in any form, whether thought or behaviour,
whether visual or written].
Every *other* sin that a man commits is outside the body,
but the one who is sexually immoral sins against his own body.

1. How I Got "Behind the Windows of a Smile"

In 1979 in a world of sin, my mother gave birth to me. I'm sure I was my parents' pride and joy—after all, I was their firstborn. They raised me in church, and we were active members of our local assembly. Many people have told me stories of how adorable I was and that everyone wanted to hold me. I'd say they were right; everyone wanted to hold me and mold me, including Satan. He saw me when I was conceived and put together a scheme to destroy my life.

The biggest reason for Satan wanting to hold me was because I was a female. Satan hates women because, in the time of Adam, Genesis 3:15 NLT says: "And I will cause hostility between you and the woman, and between your offspring and her offspring. He will strike your head, and you will strike his heel."

Because a woman can bring life and our enemy comes to steal, kill and destroy life, I believe that when the devil saw my body enter the world, he knew that God had a plan for my life as an individual. The enemy had a purpose and had to do his best to steal my purpose. He knew I had a praying mother and father and also knew I had potential from the start. He knew I was "fearfully and wonderfully made," as Psalm 139:14 NKJV says, but he had to figure out a plan to take away as much of my potential as he could at the earliest time possible in my life.

When I was growing up, life was good. It was just me, mom and dad. I was well taken care of and had no cares in the world. When I was four, my brother was born. He was the cutest little thing ever. Our parents decided we needed more space with a growing family, so we moved to the house where my childhood fun and care-free days would end.

My life had had a great start. My family was very hospitable and was always offering help to those in need. We always had guests over for various reasons, and often offered them a place to stay. We had lots of family get-togethers, and many shared fellowship and dined with us. From the outside, my life would have seemed so normal.

We had a pastor living next door. They had kids, and my brother and I played with them. They had a swing in their backyard, so we went over to play and push each other on the swing. The swing would lift into the air each time we pushed each other too hard, but we had such fun. Other times, we'd go into my house and get all the fruit we could get together, cut it up, put it on a tray and have what we called a "tutti-fruity party." As a family, we spent time together and when we had birthday parties, they were big. We used to go on family outings annually in the summer to Center Island, Wonderland, and Carnivals. Those days were a lot of fun with some of my childhood's most pleasant memories.

This leads me to the first time I know the devil tried to strip away my potential and steal from my life.

When I was five, the devil manipulated a man's mind and allowed him to be unable to tame his fleshly desires. I cannot recall exactly when this person moved in with us, but I know my parents were good friends with him; they trusted him to take me places and gave him a room to stay in next door to my brother's and my rooms.

Encounters, enticement or endearments?

My mindset in regards to these experiences was trusting because the people that I experienced sexual abuse from were people that I trusted and believed were trustworthy. They were not strangers, they were friends and family. I didn't have any expectation that any of them would do anything wrong to me or encourage me to do things that were not right or good for me. My perception and belief in them were through the eyes of a child. As described in Matthew 18:3 (AMP), the Bible talks about having childlike faith that is completely trusting, humble and forgiving. A child's trust and dependence is without reservation from a place of innocence, the mindset and perception of a child is usually complete and total trust without question.

I can remember wondering, *What are you doing? I'm tired.* I was young; I just wanted to sleep; I was tired from the day's activities. We usually played all day at school and when we got home, we would play a little more, so by the end of the day, I was tired. I was taught that night times were for sleeping.

But my restful nights began to be disrupted. He would quietly enter my bedroom at night and put his genitals by my face and feel for my hand to hold and grope him. Encounters came when I least expected them for the first few years. I couldn't see what I was doing, but I could hear him saying, "Shhh, shh." I am sure I kept quiet because I was a kid, and kids are supposed to obey adults.

These interactions taught me that my feelings didn't matter. Through my culture I had already learned that children were seen and not heard even before the abuse began. As a result I went along with what happened to me without understanding that it was not okay. As I got older, he began fondling and dry humping me.

I had become familiar with the body parts I touched, and that touched me, but something did not feel right. The abuse had begun at such a young age that it seemed normal in my childhood eyes. However, as I grew up, I began to have a clearer understanding that it was not right. I could remember what I felt and what it felt like, yet I couldn't say anything, and I did not understand why. Later in life, I learned that this pattern of behaviour has a name—grooming.

"Grooming" is when someone builds a relationship, trust, and emotional connection with a child or young person and the adults around that child so they can manipulate, exploit and abuse the child. The offender may assume a caring role, befriend the child and their family, or exploit their position of trust to groom the child and/or the child's family. They often intentionally build relationships with the adults around the child or seek a less supervised child, which increases the likelihood that their time with the child is welcomed and encouraged.

The purpose of grooming has many fronts. It is to manipulate the perceptions of other adults around the child, to manipulate the child into becoming a cooperative participant, to reduce the chances of the child being believed if they do disclose the abuse, and to reduce the likelihood of the abuse being detected (National Society for the Prevention of Cruelty to Children, 2021).

The six stages of sexual grooming

1. Choosing a Victim

    The predator often chooses a child who is vulnerable. Children who are withdrawn, low in confidence, emotionally deprived or have less parental supervision are particularly at risk. At night, my parents, the parents of two young children, were tired from work, which left me vulnerable to my abuser as he was often in our home.

2. Building Access and Trust

    Sexual abuse often begins with a friendship. The abuser can also take on other roles such as a romantic partner, mentor, caregiver or even authority figure. The abuser spends time getting to know the victim's likes, dislikes and habits and pretends to share common interests. The abuser can be a friend or family member; it is not limited to being a stranger.

3. Filling a Need with Gifts and Favours

    Perpetrators give the victim small gifts and favors to make the child feel indebted. Trust is enhanced by sharing intimate life details, going on special outings and giving the child access to drinks, drugs or cigarettes, depending on the child's age. In my case, I was enticed with toys, candies, McDonald's—whatever it took, whatever I asked for—so that, in the end, I would freely fulfill his needs since I felt a sense of obligation to do whatever he asked of me.

4. Isolating

The groomer actively tries to isolate the child from people who may be watchful or helpful (such as parents or siblings). This kind of isolation creates more profound connection and dependency. The offender exhibits exemplary behaviour in front of the victim's parents and manipulates them into trusting the relationship. That reduces the likelihood of a disclosure and increases the likelihood that the child will repeatedly return to the offender. I was treated exceptionally well by this person, but it was not out of pure kindness, fondness, care or because the person loved me. It was out of manipulation in order to build trust so he could continue to sexually abuse me and keep me silent.

5. Sexualizing or Desensitizing to Touch

This is the stage before the actual abuse. The abuser increases non-sexual touching to prepare the child for the abuse. This may include hugs, snuggles and tickling. The offender creates situations involving nudity (swimming, massages, watching pornography) where the adult exploits the child's natural curiosity and uses sexual stimulation to excite the child and advance abuse.

When a child is sexually abused or touched inappropriately for the purpose of sexual arousal, they learn many things outside the field of true or clear understanding. I learned to dry hump without knowing what it was until I got to my later teenage years—and developed an even clearer perspective of

11

it in the process of writing this book. I prematurely learned the texture of an adult male penis touching my face and body.

6. Secrecy and Maintaining Control

The offender uses emotional blackmail and blame to advance to the sexual relationship and maintain its secrecy. The offender warns the victim no one will believe them if they open up and that the victim was the one who "started it." I developed a false sense of obligation to the abuser, but he used these tactics to prevent me from speaking up. If I said I was going to tell, he would remind me of all the things he had given me and what we had done and tell me that he would lose his job if I told.

That is not love

When the sexual abuse started, I was being taught many things prematurely by that flawed person. The acts displayed by his corrupted lifestyle and mindset helped build my formative belief systems and values while smearing my lens of perception.

This situation brought so much confusion into my life, as all I could hear was endearment; he always said he loved me.

1 Corinthians 13:4-8a says: "[4]Love suffers long and is kind; love does not envy; love does not parade itself, is not puffed up; [5] does not behave rudely, does not seek its own, is not provoked, thinks no evil; [6] does not rejoice in iniquity, but rejoices in the truth; [7] bears all things, believes all things, hopes all things, endures all things.[8] Love never fails."

However, when someone takes advantage of you, that is not love. I remember being given almost anything that I wanted as a child. Was it just because he wanted to bless me with nice things, or was there more to it? No one ever questioned his motives that I'm aware of, but how I wish someone had. As I got older, I lived to appease this man so I could get the treats and toys, not realizing I was doing what he wanted.

In this way, my interactions with this abuser altered my perception of what love is supposed to look like. Anger began to grow within me because I didn't know how to express what I was feeling. I was filled with questions for him: *Why do you keep waking me up in the dark? Why do you only do this to me in the dark when I go to sleep?*

When I got to my adult years, the thing that most sharply concerned me and brought the most intense questioning to my mind was, *Why didn't I tell or say something to anyone at five, six or seven years old?* But he was a grown-up—I felt that if I told my parents, they would believe him, the adult, because children then were seen but not heard.

I've always heard it said that children talk too much, but in my experience, that is not true, especially when a child is being groomed.

Underlying anger

Growing up, I was an active child. I interacted well with other children and enjoyed playing with them, but I was unhappy and angry inside. When I was playing with my friends and playmates, my underlying anger would cause me to switch from play-fighting to real fighting in an instant, which would confuse them and even myself.

I remember going to school and beating up on boys for no real reason at all. Looking back, I can remember a time in grade one when out of nowhere, I picked up a little boy and body-slammed him to the ground. When he hit the floor, I wondered in my mind what I'd done. I remember seeing him cry when he hit the floor and when I looked at his back it was black and blue. I couldn't even say why I did it because I didn't know myself. He cried and said, "I'm going to tell the principal on you." I begged and pleaded with him not to, but he did. I don't blame him; I would have done that too. I didn't even have a reason to body-slam him—after all, he didn't do anything to me— or did I?

It seemed as if I had no reason for doing such a terrible thing to this innocent little boy whose complexion highlighted his injuries. Could there have been an underlying issue I was dealing with as a young child? Could there have been an underlying issue I could not make sense of because I was so young?

The windows of a smile

Days and nights went by, months and even years of this sexual abuse continued producing confusing ideas and views in my life.

Let me take you behind the windows of a smile. I fought boys because they were boys and the person who was harassing me at night was a "boy," a bigger one I could not stop. Due to the helplessness that I experienced at home, seeds of anger began to sprout in my life. Later in life, I had to recognize and re-learn not to categorize all boys or men as selfish people who just wanted to violate me.

From that first sexual attack, I learned to hate without even knowing what hate was, and I began suppressing my feelings because I was keeping a secret. I learned about things I should not have learned about until I could consent to know about them.

Because I was a child, that happened without my consent or understanding of the true nature of the perpetrator's acts—or his intentions. In the same way that the devil is sly and deceiving in an adult's life, the devil and the abuser deceive the child into believing that what the abuser is doing is right. It is said that what a child experiences in their early childhood days lasts forever. That is why the Bible tells us to "train up a child in the way he/she should grow: and when he is old, he will not depart from it" (Proverbs 22:6 KJV).

Peer abuse

Then there was an unexpected twist to my story—another abuser entered my life when I was eight; he was a teenager.

This is an example of peer abuse, abuse by another child who is three or more years older, has a substantial developmental difference or greater physical size.

This experience differed from the first one, as this abuser was a relative; I automatically trusted him because of the family connection. I didn't have any reason to believe anything he wanted to do with me would be wrong. Another major difference was that he used a lot more force and was aggressive in his approach.

He would come by to visit, however, without wanting to truly visit my family. He was never really interested in playing with my brother and me. His interest seemed to be about getting sexual pleasure from "playing" with me or doing what he wanted to get satisfaction from me even though I didn't want to "play" those detestable games with him. It seemed strange to me that he always wanted to play with me alone.

I remember very clearly that it started with him forcing me to watch pornography. He'd say, "Let's watch a movie," but then I'd realize it was not a movie I wanted to see. It wasn't a children's movie or show; it was for adults. I didn't want to see it, so I would try to move away, but he would hold me down, cover my mouth and pry my eyes open to force me to watch it. When I threatened to tell on him, he would cover my mouth, so I couldn't say a thing and no one could hear me. When I said, "No!" or "Stop!" or "I'm telling!" he would say, "No!"

This went on for a while. It escalated to him calling me into my parents' room to play in a detestable way. When I asked him why we were going in their room or what we were going to do, he said, "Let's play house."

When I said "No," he'd persuade me by saying, "Come on," and I'd agree.

When he told me to lie on the bed, and he started pulling my pants and underwear off, I asked him, "Why do I have to take my clothes off?" Then he started touching my vagina and trying to insert his fingers into it. I told him it was hurting, and I'd push his hand away from the area, telling him to stop. But he'd use more force and tell me to be quiet. So I pushed him and tried to call out to my parents, but he got up quickly and ran away. This happened on more than one occasion.

16

At other times, he'd try to take off my clothes in a dark room while groping me and rubbing his groin area on my private places. I was frustrated and hurt. But he wouldn't stop forcing me to do things I didn't want to do or lying to me about what we were going to play to isolate me in an area.

My voice wasn't heard

He didn't even hear me crying out, "Stop!" or maybe he ignored my voice. It made me feel like I had no voice. Although I was begging for him to stop, he didn't care because what I wanted did not matter. I was just an object for his gratification. I often wondered, *Where are my parents? Why can't they catch us so this can stop? Why can't this stop?* Then I began to wonder, *Do all families play this way?*

Some might suggest it was kids being curious, but I was not curious. I did not want to play the games he started and wanted to play.

I wanted to play normal games using toys, playing tag or hide-and-seek. I wondered, *Why does he always say, "Let's watch a movie," as if it's a cartoon or a fun movie and then show me these naked people? Maybe it's a fun or exciting movie for him to watch, so he assumes I will enjoy it too.*

At the onset of these interactions, he didn't listen to me. I was upset because he ignored me when I said, "No!" or "Stop!" As the interactions increased over time, my strength increased too. So, if we were playing and he did something I didn't want him to do or that hurt me, I began to fight back and get him off of me physically.

I was tormented by the fact that I was forced to do what I didn't want to do until, in some strange way, I found some pleasure in what I didn't ask for. I thought something must be wrong with me. *Why do people always want to touch my private parts when I don't ask them to and when I don't show off my body to get their attention? Is something wrong with me? Why don't they listen to me when I say "No!" or "Stop!"? Why do I have to fight them off? Why do they do this to me and to no one else?* I remember being so angry at him that I wanted to cut his head off and put it on a platter.

He didn't hear my voice and my words didn't matter to him, but God heard them and they mattered to HIM. One day, as suddenly as they had begun, the inappropriate and detestable actions came to an end. I don't think I offered him the satisfaction he desired, and that was okay with me. I later found out he continued the same pattern with another relative.

I told some of my friends, but at the same time, I also told them not to tell anyone because I feared the outcome. I believed it wasn't my fault when my friends told me so, but I didn't know how to stop the abuse.

The toughest reality

The toughest reality for me to face was that there were some pleasurable moments, while most of the things done to me made me feel horrible and violated and created a sense of distrust.

Resentment and anger began to rest deep within my heart. I was terribly disturbed by the thought that I could find some pleasure in such an act. I felt so disturbed that I thought I'd be better off dead. I didn't want to live, but I couldn't die. So, I started attempting

18

suicide to end my own life because I didn't feel worthy of living. I was afraid to cut myself, so death wouldn't come that way. Instead, I tried to starve myself.

Around this age, my dad stopped hugging me. I assume now it was because he thought I was grown. Had he known what had happened to me at the hands of the abusers, perhaps he would have had a different response, but I interpreted it as rejection. I eventually talked on the phone to many guys to keep myself distracted from the confusion and despair I was feeling.

Out in the open

I finally started to understand that what had been done to me wasn't acceptable—when it had started and while it continued. When it started, I didn't know it was wrong, but as I got older, I knew it wasn't right.

Something made me afraid to tell, hesitant to tell my parents. Maybe it was the enemy urging me not to tell so the abuse would be prolonged. I'll never forget the day I told my best friend about what had happened to me. She was so angry, she snapped. She couldn't believe that I was fourteen, and this had been going on since I was five. She was angry, but she was a child too, so when I begged her not to tell anyone, she didn't.

Then, one day I told an adult family friend about the first abuser. She didn't do what the others had done when I pleaded with her not to tell. I was depressed and cried about what had happened to me, but that day someone was going to stand up for me.

She changed my life. She called my father first and told him what had happened. Later that day, my father told my mother. The

19

next day my father sat with me and asked me what had happened and if it was true. I answered, "Yes," with tears in my eyes.

I was afraid of what would happen to me if the molester found out that I had told. Why was I afraid? I'm not sure. Maybe I misguidedly felt I was betraying the predator.

My parents took me to a doctor's office to check things out. The Children's Aid Society became involved. The molester was brought in and questioned. I was still afraid about what he would do to me. He was upset and seemed worried. It seemed to me he was mostly concerned about his job and reputation because he would lose his job if they were informed he was a pedophile.

I can remember one specific question they asked me at the age of fourteen: "Should we charge him or not?" I battled inside, wanting to say, "Yes," but I looked at him sitting across the table from me, staring at me with an upset look in his eyes, and then I said, "I'm not sure." Then I said, "No."

I said that because I didn't want him to be upset with me— we were part of the same community, after all. If he were charged, everyone would know what had happened. I said no because I was afraid; he was looking at me from across the large table and whispered under his breath that he was disappointed in me and wondered how I could do that to him.

It didn't even occur to him that it was open to me to say in return, "I could say the same thing about you, sir."

Something within me was still dependent on him and needed his approval. Still, even more, I wanted this twisted relationship severed. It was preventing me from living a normal child's life. In my adolescent mind, I felt as if it was wrong to charge him or tell on him. A consistent foundation of grooming and bribery was the only thing I knew, so it was kind of strange to think of charging him or that he might go to jail; he was like family.

When I got home, my father asked me, "Do you want him to stay here? Or do you want him to leave?" Initially, I said, "I don't know," then I said, "No, Dad, I don't want him to stay here. Please let him leave," as I felt insecure and needed to feel safe and have a sense of security.

That was the first time I told my dad what I wanted, that I wanted the molester to leave. Usually, I second-guessed myself and did not say what I really wanted. But this time, I knew I had to say what I really wanted as my decision would affect me for life. I needed this dysfunctional relationship to stop.

As any protective father would, my father told him he had to leave. Despite them being close friends, my father had to do what was in his child's best interests.

Nothing that happened at that time was spoken about again. It was like our little family secret. Only the people that dealt with the situation knew about it, so no one else in the family knew as it was not talked about.

Being silenced in that way created additional layers of secrecy that ultimately added even more trauma for me.

Other molesters

The third person who abused me was the male friend of a relative.

I used to stop by to eat lunch at their house because it was easier and cheaper than buying lunch at school. I would get to see their kids and play with them, then go back to school. I thought I had a good friendship with him; I looked up to him as my elder.

He encouraged me about school and life, telling me to keep my head up. He told me I could talk to him about anything. At fourteen, I thought, *Wow, I have someone in my corner who knows a lot about life that I can talk to.* I talked to him about the boys at school that were making passes at me, and he told me how to deal with them. I took his advice and learned how to stand up for myself. I enjoyed talking to him, and he told me to be careful of the guys out there.

One day, he showed me a book about sexual positions when he was talking to me about boys. I told him I wasn't planning on having sex any time soon and was therefore not interested in it. This brought a shift in our relationship, but I didn't think much of it. Despite being in harm's way, I didn't realize that danger was around the corner.

One hot spring day, I went over to have lunch as usual. As I was sitting down to eat, I said to myself out loud, "I'm so hot." I was wearing a button-up top, which didn't seem revealing or enticing in any way—at least that is what I thought.

He said, "Do you want me to get the fan?"

I said, "Yes," and he brought it. Then he came over to me and tried to open one of the buttons on my top.

"What are you doing?" I asked him and started to button it back up. As I was buttoning it, he started trying to open another one. Then I pulled away and told him, "Leave my shirt; I'm not hot!"

He then picked me up and carried me to his room while I was telling him to put me down. He put me on his bed. I had candy in my mouth at the time, and he started saying, "Give me a piece of your candy."

I said, "No!" but then he tried to kiss me. I turned my face away and again said, "No," while I kept trying to push him off of me. But he was so heavy I couldn't. Then I started begging him, "Please don't do this to me. Please don't do this to me. Please don't do this to me…" over and over until he got off of me.

"I would never do anything to hurt you," he said. At that moment, his kids came home, and that's how God saved me from possibly being raped, but I was afraid.

In that situation, once again, I learned not to trust men. No matter how nice they seemed or how much they looked like they had my best interests at heart, it didn't mean that they did.

It made me so confused because it didn't make sense to me that my relative's friend would want me even when I wasn't interested in him. After all, I was just a teenager, and he was a grown man. If my own relative's friend could do that to me when he already had a woman then, what did that say about the others? As a result of these experiences, I found it hard to believe anything males would say to me or about me.

The worst part about the situation was that later that day, I called my relative and told her what happened, and she didn't believe me. He told her he didn't do anything to me. The only thing I could do was stop going over for lunch to prevent another encounter.

Once again, I didn't tell my parents because I didn't want any family problems. I decided at that point that all men were dogs. I know that wasn't a healthy idea, but that's what I kept seeing and what I was experiencing.

The fourth experience I had of someone trying to take advantage of me was with a guy from my church. I was about fifteen and had grown up seeing him all the time at church. It happened when I was singing in one of my community's mass choirs. I used to get a ride home with him sometimes because we lived nearby, and it was usually late in the evening when the practice was over.

One evening after choir practice, I was feeling awfully sick; I suffered from debilitating migraines. One of the choir directors asked the young man if he could give me a ride home. He agreed, so I got into the car and laid down on the back seat. While he was stopped at a stoplight, I felt his hand touch my private area. I was in such crippling pain I could hardly push his hand away and tell him to stop. When he dropped me home, I got out of the car as quickly as I could, went into the house and straight to bed.

Throughout the week, I thought about what to do. Innumerable thoughts went through my mind about what to say or do, so I decided to talk to someone. I knew I wanted to tell, so I decided to speak with a friend about it, and he agreed with me that I should tell right away. I decided that no matter what, I was going to tell my choir director.

The following week, I told my choir director about everything that had happened and that I wouldn't take another ride from that man again. The choir director and their assistant spoke to him and did whatever they could to deal with the matter.

It felt so good that I had learned to stand up for myself. This time I hadn't kept it to myself, as I had done in the past. For the first time, I felt free and strong. I had finally found my voice. I didn't have to give power over my life to another man.

24

It takes a lot of courage to speak up. Many abused people keep it a secret. They don't want to say anything because they feel people will criticize them, look down on them, scrutinize them, or view them as disgraceful or shameful, even though it's not their fault. That's a lie! It wasn't their fault that some man couldn't control his sexual cravings.

How could it have been my fault when I was sick and resting, and this guy reached back from his driver's seat and placed his hands on my body while moving his hand to get between my legs? How rude! It's despicable, indefensible, and unconscionable to comprehend how a person can take advantage of a helpless child or a sick person.

I tried to figure out in my head what the guy was thinking but couldn't make sense of it. I probably wasn't the first person to have gone through this with him, but at least I spoke up. As years went by, lots of other girls said of him: "He's sick!" "I don't know what's wrong with that guy!" and "He needs help."

I often wondered as a believer who loved being in a church environment, where the spirit of discernment was for identifying some of these delinquents and addressing them one on one because of the God in us. I thought there were prophetic people around me, but no one seemed to handle people with disordered sexual tendencies.

A wolf cloaked in sheep's skin

Abusers use deceit. They start like a wolf cloaked in sheep's skin, then their true colours begin to show. Proverbs 27:6 (NKJV) says, "but the kisses of an enemy are deceitful." Look at Delilah in the story of Samson and Delilah, in Judges 16. The enemy was very persistent. She came with grace, pretending she liked Samson until he fell in love with her. Most of our foes don't come looking like an enemy, but they will persistently try to bring us down or get things of value from us while acting as if they have our best interest at heart. They don't care what they have to do to get what they want; perhaps they do not even recognize what they're doing to the person they're hurting. Though she slept with Samson and brought him comfort and pleasure, Delilah couldn't see beyond what she wanted, which was to know the secret of his strength and then be rewarded for it. She didn't care that she had to betray Samson to receive the monetary gain. How cruel.

One thing I know is that real enemies have no mercy. I realize now that our enemies never give up on trying to defeat and destroy us. These are spiritual enemies, as we are spiritual beings. I realize I am not always fighting the person in front of me, because I am a believer. As Ephesians 6:12 (NKJV) says, "For we do not wrestle against flesh and blood, but against **principalities**, against **powers**, against **the rulers of the darkness of this age**, against **spiritual hosts of wickedness in the heavenly places**."

In summary
1. Be careful who you have living in your home with you and your children.
2. Be aware of your children's tendencies.
3. Be aware of your children's ailments and research what could be causing them.

4. Be aware of your children's responses and why they could be angry.

5. Protect your children by teaching them to communicate openly with you. One strategy is to have a family code word your children can use if they feel unsafe.

6. Have no secrets because predators are looking for children who can keep secrets.

7. Be wary of anyone who takes too much interest in your child and spends time alone with him or her.

8. Teach your children about their bodies and not to allow anyone to touch their private parts outside of hygiene and medical reasons.

2. The Hidden Fight

How did I deal with the confusion stemming from the violation? It was so tough as I didn't know how to express myself or how to advocate for myself. I could not understand what was being done to me or why trusted people were doing those things to me. Most of all, I couldn't understand the fear that made me hesitate to tell my parents—and when I finally did, why one of my parents wouldn't believe me.

Coping Mechanisms

Coping mechanisms are the strategies people use in the face of stress or trauma to help manage painful or difficult emotions. Coping mechanisms help people adjust to stressful events while assisting them in maintaining their emotional well-being (Government of South Australia, 2020).

There are various coping mechanisms survivors of CSA use, but I will discuss the two I employed to deal with my emotions on my journey. I used anger, and the façade of a smile to deal with my emotions.

What is anger?

Anger is a natural response to perceived threats. It makes your body release adrenaline, your muscles tighten, and your heart rate and blood pressure increase. Your senses might feel more acute, and your face and hands flush. Anger becomes a problem when it is not managed in a healthy way (Mayo Clinic, 2020).

Anger is a basic human emotion experienced by all people. It is typically triggered by an emotional hurt when we perceive mistreatment, injury, or obstacles that keep us from attaining our personal goals or oppose our long-held views (MentalHelp.net, 2020).

Anger is related to the fight, flight, or freeze response of the sympathetic nervous system; it prepares humans to fight (Psychology Today, 2021b).

Why anger?

Anger is expressed when our feelings become overwhelming. It often occurs in response to other underlying issues—a sense of hopeless violation for me—and is used to deal with pain or fear. It can be a substitute emotion because it comes across more readily than other emotional reactions.

Deep within, I was angry and tormented. Tormented by being woken up in the middle of the night by the adult perpetrator disrupting and disturbing my sleep and by the relative who violated me under the guise of play. I became angry when I wasn't heard, and my feelings were ignored.

Later, that was especially the case when I was not believed by my parent, who took the perpetrator's side. A deep resentment formed in me, resulting in a rift in our relationship. There was such a profound breakdown in our communication that although we lived in the same home, we did not speak to each other for over six years, other than acknowledging each other's presence. During that time, there was a constant current of tension in our relationship and environment.

Unresolved fight

Growing up, I was a tomboy. I often got into fights, and when I fought, 90% of the fights were with boys. It was often surprising to them that such a skinny girl had so much strength in a fight. I fought because I was angry—I felt I couldn't speak out about the abuse because the abusers would be upset with me. I fought boys frequently, and any reason would do.

If I fought a boy to protect my brother because he needed my help, all my anger from what I was suppressing would come out. I would fight uncontrollably and with every bit of rage within me. When I fought, and the anger came out, the other child would be startled and afraid because they wouldn't know why or how play-fighting or a minor squabble had changed to me fighting as if for real.

I was even afraid of myself when I lashed out. However, I couldn't fight my abusers because they were much bigger and older than me. As a result, I felt intimidated and infuriated, just hoping for the day when I could stand up to them. In my mind, I killed them a thousand times.

As a teen, I recall fighting off a guy because we misunderstood each other, and when I fought him, it got to the point where he had to ask me if I was going to kill him while he was gasping for air. He had invited me to his house to watch a football game, but it was a setup, and he had other plans in mind. Shortly after I arrived, he called me to his room. When I got there, the wall was covered with a picture of a naked woman.

At that moment, I grasped that he had a different plan in mind. When he tried to push me onto his bed, and I told him, "No!"

I realized I'd have to fight to get him off of me. I started choking him with my elbow straight into the centre of his throat. He thought I was going to kill him, and maybe I would have, but God preserved me. I was so angry and filled with adrenaline and underlying anger that I scared myself. A level of strength came that wouldn't calm down until I saw he was subdued, and I could safely leave his home.

In my unresolved fight, I found myself lashing out to defend myself or when I felt a sense of alarm—and it was uncontrollable. I tried my best not to get upset and get into fights when I got into my later teenage years as I could imagine myself doing evil things to people, and I didn't want that to be a reality. Many times, because of the battles within my mind, I felt like a ticking time bomb, never knowing when I would explode. I always felt a sense of trepidation and experienced unsettling feelings within me.

I had to get help

With all that anger within me, I didn't know if I could trust myself. I hated that I could explode all of a sudden. I could flip out on my family members, friends and even my child. Usually, I was quiet and took what was being dished out to me … until I couldn't take it anymore, and then I exploded into tears, yelling or fighting, especially if someone had instigated it. And that really scared me— I didn't want to be someone who had no self-control or discipline.

I had to get help. My daughter was one reason I had to get counselling. Many things were suppressed that I needed to get out of my system.

Through counselling and prayer, eventually, I got to a place of peace. I was able to forgive when I gave my heart to the Lord and read the Lord's Prayer. "Our Father which art in heaven, Hallowed be thy name. Thy kingdom come. Thy will be done in earth, as it is in heaven. Give us this day our daily bread and forgive us our debts, as we forgive our debtors. And lead us not into temptation but deliver us from evil: For thine is the kingdom, and the power and the glory forever, Amen" (Matthew 6:9b-13 KJV).

In that prayer, I learned that I had to forgive others if I wanted God to forgive me.

Activate

Answer the following:

1. Be vigilant and aware if you see your child fighting a lot and ask them questions such as, "What is upsetting you?"
2. Identify any triggers for your anger.
3. Write down what you can do to start dealing with the triggers for your anger.
4. Take action to deal with the triggers after determining what you can do to deal with them.

3. The Façade of a Smile (The Mask)

The façade of a smile was the other coping mechanism I used. Proverbs 15:13 NKJV says: "a merry heart makes a cheerful countenance, but by sorrow of the heart the spirit is broken." Studies have shown that smiling releases endorphins, natural pain killers and serotonin, which elevate our mood (Stibich, 2021).

A smile usually expresses happiness or positive feelings. During my youth, I smiled a lot, and sometimes people asked why I was smiling. I often said, "I'm smiling because God is good to me; He made me happy and saved my life." There was truth to that, yet my answer lacked transparency. I was often smiling because it was a coping mechanism, which I used for dealing with some of the effects of the CSA I faced as a child.

Why the façade smile?

Wearing a smile made me feel less heavy. By smiling constantly, I believed people wouldn't try to find out how I really was—and that worked. While I was behind the windows of my smile, nobody really asked too many questions because everything appeared to be fine. The only issue was that I was not okay. Nevertheless, behind the windows of a smile, nobody questioned me, so I felt safe. Childhood Sexual Abuse caused such a distortion of the lens that I viewed life through.

When I smiled, I felt lighter, and the weight of my problems and the trauma I experienced decreased. Smiling covered the tears I wanted to cry, and they fell behind the smile or within it. When I smiled, I hid the hate and anger behind that mask. That helped me to let go of the frustrations awaiting me, and my heart felt lighter. The smile took away the pain and sadness for the time it was there; it brought the peace I needed to feel when I was frustrated.

I spent much of my time growing up within a church setting for choir practices, prayer services, fasting, youth services, Bible study, Sunday morning and evening services, concerts etc. It would have appeared that I was interacting freely with people, and I seemed to be reasonably social.

However, I had many apprehensions. I experienced anxiety and always felt as if bad things were about to happen in my relationships or to me. My suspicions always leaned to the negative side as there were many things in my childhood that just didn't make sense.

Wearing a smile countered what I was feeling and got me out of my head, if only for a little while. It helped me fit into the groups around me, even though I felt I didn't truly belong. No matter how much I tried, I always felt I ended up alone on the fringes of the group. I couldn't walk around with a frown, as it would only draw attention to me. The façade of a smile was necessary so I could fit in as best as possible.

In private, I was being intimidated, but I didn't know that's what was happening. Those people were bigger and older than me and knew how to manipulate me. Because of the first abuser's gifts and kindness, I often thought I was harsh in believing it was intimidation and manipulation. However, as I read, researched, had counselling sessions and prayed, I realized I was not going crazy—I was being manipulated, and I could not be silent about it anymore.

The dysfunction of the façade smile

There are many dysfunctions involved in a façade smile because it is built on pretense and deception. It causes more trust issues; others can't trust whether you're really truly expressing your feelings. Neither can you trust yourself; sometimes, you don't know whether you're putting on a show or not. Continuing to be a chameleon for everyone else drains your energy. Living deceptively is emotionally, mentally, and physically exhausting and drains your spirit as you are not doing what Romans 13:13a KJV says: "Let us walk honestly, as in the day."

I knew I could not continue hiding behind the smile; it felt more and more fake the older I got. It no longer created a safety zone for me. I felt as if I was living a lie by pretending to smile. I realized, too, that I would have to stop hiding and walk into freedom because there is liberty where the spirit of the Lord is. It was dysfunctional to live a deceptive life around people, and I didn't want to do that.

The change had to begin with me. I knew I needed to seek help, so I sought the Lord in prayer to help me in my areas of struggle. I read the Bible and prayed for wisdom about living my life functionally because I knew I couldn't do it on my own. What I found was that I had to choose to do things differently.

I had to choose to be intentional—to smile when I really wanted to, and refrain from smiling when I didn't. I also learned to be truthful, not false or fake, which then reinforced that by pretending to smile, I was lying. My smile came from a more authentic place through this process, and then I smiled with a true purpose.

35

I now know God gave me that smile and put it there for a purpose. With it, He protected me behind my fake smile and carried me when I felt I couldn't carry on. It hid the frightened, sad and insecure child looking for true unconditional love.

Hiding behind the windows of that smile brought me safety, peace and hope until I found true unconditional love in my relationship with God. And he loved me back to life.

Activate

Answer the following:
1. Why do you smile?
2. Do you have a reason to smile?
3. Write down ten things that you are thankful for that make you smile. If you can't find ten, do as many as you can find.
4. Are you fake smiling?
5. Choose to smile for a purpose and smile authentic smiles.

4. Childhood Programming Quietly Controls Your Entire Life

As we age, we should mature and better understand the things occurring in our lives. Generally, we better grasp how to deal with various relationships in our lives. However, you may find your adult perceptions are affected by childhood perceptions, solidifying into adulthood viewpoints. The early stages of growth from zero to six years are when most brain development and learning occur. That is the age where children are like sponges soaking up everything they are exposed to. As they learn and start building their core foundational values, perceptions and beliefs, repetitive experiences get embedded into the subconscious mind. Prior to the age of six, the brain is in a theta brain wave state, which is associated with a state of hypnosis. After six, the brain starts filtering brain waves.

Listening to Natalie Ledwell and Mary Morrissey's MindMovies.com video about "Success Blockers" helped me to understand that while I was going through the earliest stages of CSA, my brain was being programmed. The programming didn't start with being woken up at night but with the grooming. It now makes sense that I couldn't see the problem—I didn't even know it existed because of the previous predatory grooming. My inability to see I was in imminent danger in all the situations when I was abused also resulted from that earlier programming. Grooming normalized that behaviour for me from such a young age that I had difficulty recognizing when someone had ulterior motives.

Belief

I believed for a long time that there was something defective within me. I felt abnormal. Something inside didn't feel right.

For a long time, I wished I was a boy. I associated being a boy with getting to stay out with my friends and having more freedom than girls had. More importantly, I felt I would not have gone through what I did if I had been a boy.

When I went to middle school, I always gave guys the cold shoulder when they came around me, even those I was interested in. I always said I didn't like them even if I did. I secured myself emotionally by building protective walls around me so I wouldn't be further hurt.

I felt dirty and wasted and used. I felt like I was a waste of a body here on Earth, and it wouldn't matter if I disappeared. I didn't want to live, and I didn't know why.

Yet, I didn't say anything because I didn't know what people would think of me. No one held a gun to my head and told me not to tell anyone, but something inside me made me afraid to tell someone what I was facing and what was happening to me. I was stuck between being afraid of getting into trouble and afraid of being rejected for what had happened.

When I grew up, I learned that these are a child's built-in coping mechanisms, which become foundational attitudes when carried into adulthood. You or others might question why you deal with things a certain way but it could stem from a childhood coping mechanism for keeping yourself safe. It is said that children learn what they experience. That is certainly true when we look at the effects and traumas in the life of a person who was the victim of CSA.

Disturbing memories

A place of confusion is all I can remember—not knowing if anything was wrong or right. I couldn't figure it out.

I wished I could "unsee" the things shown to me, but I could not; I couldn't erase them. They were parts of my past, no matter what. To begin with, I wished the first perpetrator had not exposed me to the things he exposed me to.

I felt sad; I felt angry; I felt confused; I felt depressed—I felt so many things. But at the same time, I had a family who loved me, and I went to church, so I thought I couldn't be ungrateful because of these good things.

I felt as if I was missing out on a lot of the carefree times I should have had as a child and many memories as I grew up too fast and was engaged in adult activity way too early.

When I played with friends my age, some of the things we did were highly inappropriate. I had a few curiosity-driven childhood play experiences with some of my friends, girls and boys in my age group. I can remember us touching each other inappropriately and grinding on each other. I now realize that was because I was programmed wrongly at an early age, and we had curious minds. With different friends, it was different things, but thank God, that didn't last for long.

When I got to my teenage years and began to recognize right from wrong, I not only had to carry the shame and guilt of being sexually abused. I also had to deal with the shame and guilt of inappropriate childhood play. I hated myself for that.

I'm sure we were curious as kids, but we acted out what we lived and learned. The first abuser's abuse had become a part of me, and it became an addictive physical attraction. I craved things I knew I had to hide. I found myself battling as a teen with a desire for pornography, and by the early stages of teenage-hood, I found myself enacting the things I saw on the videos even though the abusers were no longer around.

From my experience and research, I have learned that CSA activates sexual desires prematurely; however, those feelings do not automatically stop because the abuse comes to an end.

I explained to my daughter that having sex or being involved in sexual activities is like eating ice cream for the first time. Before eating ice cream, you have no appetite for it, but after eating ice cream, you do. And once you have an appetite for it, you can have cravings for it, and must have it.

In other words, once you have experienced forms of sexual activity, whether it's against your will or not, your body's physiological and involuntary physical responses will give you an appetite for it. Even if the experience was painful, micro parts of it might still have given you some form of physical pleasure. Despite your lack of consent, a physiological reaction occurs.

I hated feeling that I wasn't entirely in control of those behaviours. I also struggled with masturbation to gratify my sexual cravings. That brought on further shame, guilt and depression. I found myself constantly asking God to help me stop and telling myself that I would stop, but it was a struggle.

At times when I looked at the people around me, they looked like pornographic screen images haunting me. I was continuously going to the altar for prayers. I prayed and cried at home for God to help me as I knew I couldn't do it without His help or someone else's help—I felt helpless.

I felt there must have been something wrong with me, and questions constantly swirled in my mind: *Why didn't you tell someone? Why didn't you say something to your family?* I felt ashamed, guilty and bad for having the habits, addictions, and appetite built up by the violations of these individuals.

Education and encounters

I was being manipulated like a puppet on a string while simultaneously learning to manipulate others. I didn't understand I was being manipulated—I didn't understand that until I was 41.

While being instructed to be quiet, I learned to be quiet and sneaky and keep dark secrets when the abuser was sneaking into my room at night. I learned to be woken out of my sleep and not make any noise. Because I had been taught what to do if I heard a sound or someone was coming, I learned to pretend I was doing one thing while I was doing something else—I responded as if I was not interacting sexually with the abuser. I learned these behaviours at a tender age only because the abuser had taught me.

From these encounters, I learned how to be touched by a man, how to touch a man and how to please a man. I was taught to devalue my feelings, how to be silent when told and how to exist for someone else's satisfaction.

One thing always stood out to me. At eight, my actions and responses to the sexual encounters with my adult abuser changed due to my unwanted exposure to pornography by the teen abuser. The adult perpetrator was not only not reluctant to engage in my newly learned behaviours—he welcomed them.

His actions were very upsetting, disturbing, and disappointing when I reflected on them.

Unrestrained by triggers

While going through the CSA, I encountered various triggers. A trigger is something that sets off a memory tape or flashback, transporting the person back to the occasion of the original trauma. It causes the person to experience overwhelming emotions, physical symptoms or thoughts. The intensity of the individual's emotional reaction can even result in a flashback where the memories cause fright, alarm, or guardedness (Saskatoon Sexual Assault & Information Centre, 2021).

During my life, there were times when I was forming relationships when I had major trust issues because of my underlying feelings of distrust. If someone gave me a gift or anything of value, significant or not, I felt as if they would require something of me in return. As a result, I was always reluctant to accept gifts and kindness. I constantly refused to accept them from men. I would question their motives, whether they were pure or not. I used to experience a sense of unease, and I lost my equilibrium because of the trauma.

When I was pregnant with my daughter, for example, I went to visit the doctor. During the examination, the nurse did something that was a part of the standard, normal process, but it reminded me of a traumatic and unwanted CSA experience I'd faced as a child. As a result of my response, she abruptly stopped the examination and exclaimed that my response to a routine check-up was abnormal. She'd seen how I moved away quickly and tensed up as if I was trying to protect myself from harm as if she was going to violate me when both of us knew she was only doing an examination. She asked me what was wrong.

"Nothing," I said. She replied that something was not right with my response. I was stunned and responded only with, "Umm…could it be because I was sexually abused as a child?"

"Possibly," she responded. "How did you get this way?" I told her it was different than what I'd experienced when I was younger. Nevertheless, she told me that I needed to get some help to deal with it because when I was delivering the baby, I would encounter many doctors checking my cervix for the baby's location.

I had experienced many triggers in my previous marriage and exhibited fear or panic about things that reminded me of my CSA.

There were even triggers from some types of music. They reminded me of the music on the pornographic videos I had been forced to watch. I avoided listening to that type of music to prevent myself from being taken back to those memories. Many people found that music so beautiful, and it did not trigger them. But for me, it was like a switch that activated my appetite for the sexually explicit materials I was exposed to as a young child. As I got older, I had a greater sense of self-control, so if I heard that music, I would take charge of my feelings and tell myself, *I pray Lord to remove any thoughts in my mind that are not of you and let me think on whatever things are lovely, pure, true, and of a good report* (Philippians 4:8 NKJV).

Dysfunctions must be dealt with—or else they can be triggered

When we go through CSA or other traumatic experiences, it is essential to get help and deal with the situation and the problem area. If trauma is left untreated, it can breed dysfunctional attitudes and behaviours within an individual. For instance, I stopped eating particular candies, because they were a reminder of previous Childhood Sexual Abuse and traumatic experiences. However, that didn't stop the triggers because I hadn't dealt with the problem. Even thinking about a specific type of candy used to remind me of the abuse and grooming I went through early in the CSA process. It has gotten a lot better, but please note—the most important thing is to deal with the problem from the root.

Avoidance solves nothing. As I dealt with the problem from the root, the triggers started to lessen. Doing that took effort, will and passion, so I could eventually walk in freedom. I had to face what I didn't want to face.

Mindset, perceptions and lived experience

As a result of my CSA experiences, I developed a contaminated mindset for relating with men. My perceptions were always clouded and blurred by the old threat of, "If you don't do this, you cannot have that."

I'd been strategically manipulated and hadn't recognized it. I'd deeply trusted the first abuser as he was around me all the time, and my family had a very close relationship with him. I didn't feel any threat of imminent physical violence from him. However, the manipulative threat was still there, the treat that if I didn't come here or go there with him, I wouldn't get a particular treat. So, I complied and then I got the treat. My lived experience was based on getting what I was coaxed to do, not what I wanted. I continued behaving that way because it had become a normalized part of my life. His grooming and the consistency of the encounters made the behaviour part of me.

Pleasing the adult abuser as a child taught me that men were untrustworthy, that people sometimes used kindness as a tool to gain control and get me to go along with what they wanted without being clear about their true intent.

Within adult relationships with men, I reacted based on the flashbacks about the persuasion and badgering I had experienced as a child and teen—and ultimately, I would just give in to their demands after many refusals, even though that was not what I truly wanted.

In adult relationships, I often compromised and agreed when I should not have. I thought that doing something to make the other person happy would make our relationship stand the test of time. I found out along the way that was not true, though. I had to learn to perceive that my happiness was just as valuable as that of others.

Revictimization

As I got older, the madness began. I felt out of place and wondered to myself, *Am I stupid, naïve, ignorant, ugly? A sex object or just foolish? Why do I always align myself with tough guys? Guys, who don't care about me as an individual or my feelings?*

45

I realized that, as a child, I'd experienced people who didn't value my feelings or hear my voice. I was gravitating to what I knew, as it was deeply ingrained within my subconscious and was quietly controlling my life.

I felt so frustrated with myself at times because I couldn't tell who had good intentions towards me, even if they did. In the long run, I suffered the consequences of careless and confusing choices, which led to a maddening and frustrating thought—did I have a sign on my forehead saying, *Come and abuse me; do what you want with me.* I wondered, *Am I a magnet for abuse?*

I experienced sexual harassment or abuse on various occasions when it felt as if people had the right to take advantage of me. Whether it was due to my size or something else, I just couldn't figure it out. My hope, though, was that I would stop attracting abuse to myself.

As I got into my adult years, I learned about revictimization (Fadelici, 2020). This happens when a person who has survived Childhood Sexual Abuse is victimized again. According to Psychology Today, "a child who is abused is at a significantly higher risk of being revictimized in adolescence and adulthood" (Engel, 2019). Anna Jaffe and her fellow researchers summarized the situation as: "The most consistent predictor of future trauma exposure is a history of prior trauma exposure" (Jaffe *et al.*, 2019). Childhood Sexual Abuse is among the strongest predictors of continued victimization (Mohammed, 2015).

I was swamped with a lot of unforgiveness, bitterness and resentment toward the abusers so I decided to get into boxing. By learning to box, I thought I could channel my anger and protect myself from any future abuse. When I went to the lessons, I hoped another female would be there, so that I wouldn't feel like a spectacle. Eventually, another young woman came, and that was definitely comforting.

I started thinking of quitting, though, because of winter and how early it got dark. Then one cold, dark winter evening, my coach offered me a ride. I accepted as I had already missed the last bus to my area. I sat and waited for my coach, and when the last person left, he went to the office to get his things. When he came out, supposedly ready to close the gym, I started to get up from the chair and reached back to get my bag. My coach then braced himself against me, and I fell back in the chair. I was surprised and asked what he was doing. He didn't reply but just continued pushing himself against me while told him, "No!" Then he tried to kiss me. "No! Please, just drop me home." In my heart, I was asking God to please protect me, and asking why this was happening to me again and by my coach now.

As a result of that experience, I quit boxing and never went back; that was the end of my wanting to be a professional boxer. Thinking about it now, I realize that was probably not the direction God had for my life. This is an example of revictimization and how the cycle of abuse continues in the lives of people who have been abused. It's as if you just subconsciously attract abusers.

Many children/adolescents disassociate from others and tend to isolate themselves to be in control or as a protective mechanism because of their lack of trust. However, that leaves them vulnerable to revictimization because they are disassociated from those who can protect them. This is why childhood abuse should not be dealt with alone.

The pain and brokenness behind my façade of a smile was a combination of the memories and madness I experienced in life.

Unravelling the carpet: family conversations

Secrecy is not as simple as the abuser whispering to the child-victim. It mostly goes deeper and is not within the child's control, especially when the child is being groomed. Abusers use secrecy and blackmail to keep the child from telling others, like their parents, about their encounters. Abusers may tell the child no one will believe them, so the child feels afraid to talk to their parents.

Parents, you are your child's superheroes, the ones your child should feel safest and most secure with. It is vital to listen to your children and believe them when they come to you and tell you their truth. When children tell you about sexual abuse, it is usually true. It is extremely difficult to talk about going through abuse. Consequently, it is best if you let them know they are valuable to you. Take the time to understand them and don't shut them down by telling them it's not true. Reassure them that you want to know what happened so you can help them. The same applies to any adult who is made aware of CSA.

My parents and siblings have not—as of my time of writing this—had a conversation about this together. The only time my parents discussed the abuse with me was when we went to the Children's Aid Society. At other times, they were small conversations with either my mom or dad. As much as I wanted, I couldn't just shut up and die, so now and then, it would come up for me and I would bring it up with my mother because it felt open-ended.

In pulling the carpet's strings and unravelling it, there was no easy moment for dealing with what happened. After all, he was a close family friend, and how could he have done such a terrible thing? So now when I address the CSA I can do so with greater insight and knowledge as to why this person was so close to and so kind to my parents amidst what was, said, done or believed. Being unwilling to unravel the carpet and talk about those intricate situations your child has faced creates an obstacle that hinders the development and advancement of the child's life.

Let us begin to unravel the carpets and have the family conversations needed to no longer settle for living in pretense and dissatisfaction.

Conversations my family won't have

The last time I spoke to my mom about the abuse was while the first abuser was also present. He said, "Please, let her stop bringing this up; it has been dealt with before." He apologized again, but I didn't feel settled within.

My mom told me to stop bringing it up by saying, "That's enough. We've talked about this before." But I wasn't okay with it, and no matter how I tried not to bring it up, it still bothered me.

I realize now that I continued being bothered by what happened because triggers and trauma don't disappear with a few contrite words—or even with time.

Talking about the abuse was treated as if I was trying to bring shame and disgrace to my family for something I wasn't even responsible for. Or as if I was seeking revenge on the abusers. Those were not, and would never be, my motives for speaking or sharing my story.

Oh, the injustice of older and bigger people taking advantage of a child!

Being set free

However, the windows of a smile must be opened so we can begin to understand each other and walk in true love and freedom. How can we ever have a truly functional family if we are afraid of being honest and authentic with each other, especially with those who are supposed to be the closest to us? How can we say we love each other and not be honest with each other because of fear of harsh judgment? Or fear of no understanding or willingness to hear each other out? Or fear of having no chance to explain how we truly feel? We cannot always be right about everything; each person should always be learning and growing in their understanding of life.

In a functional family, we learn at times how to relate functionally with each other. There is no perfect person or family, so I implore you families to take the time to have these conversations. One of them could save a life and help your loved one to step out from behind the windows and cage of the façade smile and walk in freedom from the bondage of secrecy. Your loved one may have been in that bondage for a year, five years, twenty years, thirty years, however long.

It isn't easy to live a life where you can't just be yourself. It is painful not to be able to speak about the things hurting you or to set limitations, so you don't offend another. The secrecy compounds the pain of the abuse.

Children, no matter their age, are told to "honour your father and mother which is the first commandment with a promise attached" (Ephesians 6:2 KJV). I think that honouring your father and mother means being honest with them in a loving manner; it is something we should all be able to do.

However, I know that not every culture is willing to embrace the truth because the truth often hurts. There is a saying the truth causes offence, nevertheless "…the truth shall make you free" (John 8:32b KJV). It is a beauty to see families walking in freedom, honesty and loyalty to each other instead of feeling gagged to say nothing and keep their mouths shut.

5. Filtering Thoughts, Trauma and Tribulation

Eventually, I began filtering through my thoughts, trauma and tribulation. Probing them, walking through them and living them was a truly challenging process.

Courage over fear, anger and guilt

The further I journeyed, the more I realized I was also a hurt victim, and as I got older, I gained more understanding of what I had lived through.

As a child, my anger turned into anguish; I suffered mentally and experienced pain. I remember having headaches so often that my friends didn't even want me around at times because I always ended up getting sick and crying much of the time. A sense of anguish that no one could help me hovered over me.

I remember being filled with the pain and suffering from keeping a secret; my mind was constantly under pressure because I wanted to tell but felt obligated not to. I was often yelled at, which also gave me a tendency to live in fear and nervousness about speaking up, especially about things I didn't want to do.

I had to have more courage than the fear I felt, so I could take a step toward creating a monumental change in my life, but as a young teen, I couldn't do that on my own.

The first step was to open my mouth and speak. However, for most of my life, I didn't say much unless I felt free to speak. I told some of my friends, but I also told them not to tell as I was afraid of getting in trouble or causing conflict.

I was angry at myself, too, because I felt I must be a coward for not speaking up even though I could talk to my friends. And I was angry because I did things that I didn't want to do. I felt guilty because I hadn't said something or told an adult earlier.

Finally, I realized I was exhibiting my suppressed anger and irritability with my family and relationships and saw the continuing effect the trauma was having on me.

I became a fighter—I had to fight for my life and the lives of my generation. I couldn't continue to live as a hurt victim. It was even affecting my health through chronic migraines.

The first step I took toward fighting for victory in my life was to go for personal counselling. Another step was to seek inner healing. I went on a three-day weekend retreat with a ministry team called Walking in Wholeness. At the retreat I learned I had suppressed anger and fear. They were eventually displaced in the prayer and deliverance part of the service; I remember feeling the anger leaving my body when the strong raging cry, uncontrollable screeching, screaming and wailing departed from my body. It was not high-pitched and felt like it was coming from my most profound depths. During the prayer session, I was assured that God was with me, even though we didn't go through an in-depth talk about CSA.

From that day forward, I chose to be a victor instead of a victim. I chose to walk in wholeness instead of in broken and fragmented pieces.

Doing that didn't change my thought patterns overnight—that was a process. With low self-esteem, disquietude and self-hate, living as a victor was very challenging for me as I continued wallowing in thoughts of self-pity.

Letting go of self-pity

I had to let go of self-pity and constant woe-is-me feelings. I had to choose to stop wallowing in *Why-me, poor-me, why-did-this-have-to-happen-to-me* and *where-was-God-when-this-happened-to-me?* Self-pity didn't help and kept me feeling depressed and frustrated, like a loser and sorry for myself. When I realized my plight, I knew I didn't want to remain like that, so I had to let go of those feelings, oppressing my mind, emotions and even my health.

I battled for a long time with such thoughts in my head. Eventually, my thinking became, *They've already stolen enough from my life secretly, so I will not give them the privilege of robbing me of another fragment of my life again. Now that I am an adult, no one can subject me to anything like that again because I am wiser, and I have God on my side.*

Unresolved play

Is everything okay? No, absolutely not! I still fight each and every day to be okay.

I suppressed those experiences for so long that I've had to make myself okay. Many times, I feel like I am walking around with a heavy burden. I can't tell anyone about that part of my childhood because it was so wrong. When I think about my childhood, for every good memory, there's a bad one.

Even today, as I embrace the goodness of God, I ask myself, *Am I okay?* I know I have forgiven, and I know I am healed. But I

TONYA KING

still have days when I feel disturbed about some of my childhood experiences, but I choose not to give another day of mind-wandering anxiety to the people who caused so much damage and pain in my life. Instead, I continue to unlearn and rewire as I place my hands in the hands of my Father and Maker, God.

I believe that something is wrong with molesters and abusers and they need help. Not only help—they need Jesus. Everyone needs Jesus. Jesus is the life-changer—He changed mine. Jesus is the healer, the redeemer, the deliverer, the mind-renewer. Jesus is the friend to the friendless. Jesus can restore your soul like He restored mine. Jesus is the fixer-upper—He takes broken lives and the pieces and makes them into a masterpiece.

He even mended the broken pieces of my life and made me beautiful. God is love, and the world needs the light of His love. The world needs love to be saved from sin, and the only one who can save us from sin is Jesus, the one who shed His blood and died to save mankind. John 3:16 NKJV says: "For God so love the world that He gave His only begotten son, that whoever believes in Him should not perish but have everlasting life."

It can't be dealt with alone—you don't just get over it

Childhood Sexual Abuse is real—it is serious. It's not a joke or something you deal with just by yourself. I tried to do that, but its effects were too alarming. As a child, youth—even as an adult—it shouldn't be dealt with alone.

When people are forced to deal with it alone, because of societal or cultural expectations that they will get over it, they just suppress their thoughts and feelings and "move on." But how can

55

they keep silent when they have so much to let out? Should they walk around in anger, waiting to explode? Should they just shut up and die?

I've heard that sentiment among people within my circle. "Get over it, Tonya," they say, or "How long are you going to talk about it? Let it go." Oh, how I wished I could have just gotten over it! It was so difficult given how much suppressed trauma I had. I had been bombarded by experiences I wasn't ready for.

Because of my age, things were muddled, and I often felt as if the abuse was my fault. However, after going through my thoughts, pulling up my past roots to write this book and getting information to help me understand, I realize it was not my fault. Even as I write, I sometimes still hold back tears, but I know I am delivered and marching through the process of keeping my freedom, peace and joy every day.

It is so refreshing to be bold enough to find out the truth about what I went through finally. Had I not been researching for this book, I would have never known that I had been groomed. Even though I knew something was wrong and it could not have been my fault if someone sexually abused me from the age of five, I still told myself that some of it was my fault because I didn't do anything to stop it. I could not just "get over it," and it is only God that has helped me to make it thus far. He kept me in my right mind.

I know every day is a journey to freedom, and I really hope that I will continue walking in complete freedom after the launch and release of this book. On many occasions, I didn't even want to write this, but I know for sure that I went through those hardships to have a testimony to share with you.

Don't let people derail your healing process by telling you that you should just "get over it." Whoever experiences triggers knows they don't just go away. Neither does trauma without deliverance and healing ministry and counselling or therapy. Only God can help us with undoing and unlearning the trauma.

Become a victor instead of a victim

Throughout the writing of this book, I found myself constantly saying to myself, *You have to make a choice.*

Life is about making choices, and I chose to be a victor instead of a victim. You can actively choose to be a victor and defeat your spiritual, emotional and physical enemies. Survivors often don't notice they have been drained until they realize they are crushed in spirit. "A merry heart does good, *like* medicine, but a broken spirit dries the bones" (Proverbs 17:22 NKJV).

Living with a broken spirit sucks the life, joy and energy out of a person. Living a life of defeat is no fun at all, so I ask you to consider taking back your life, your voice and every single thing stolen from you. You do that by choosing to be a victor instead of a being victim. Choose to win today. You are not alone—God is here, I am here, intercessors are here, counsellors are here, psychologists are here—you don't have to make this journey alone.

Step out from behind the walls of fear and anxiety

I had to choose to step out from behind the walls of fear and anxiety when I wanted to tell my parents. The thought of doing that created an unsettled feeling inside; my chest tightened with fear because I didn't know if they would believe me, and I feared my abuser getting mad at me.

I knew I couldn't live in fear forever and learned as I got older that God saw everything. I had to trust Him and His Word that perfect love drives out fear. "There is no fear in love; but perfect love casts out fear because fear involves torment. But he who fears has not been made perfect in love" (1 John 4:18 NKJV).

I had to trust God, hold His hand and ask Him to help me escape from behind the walls of fear and anxiety. A scripture that helped me with the anxiety was, and continues to is the one that says, "Be anxious for nothing, but in everything by prayer and supplication, with thanksgiving, let your requests be made known to God; and the peace of God, which surpasses all understanding, will guard your hearts and minds through Christ Jesus" (Philippians 4:6-7 NKJV).

6. The Empowering Journey to Becoming a Victor

This journey of empowerment involves the three Fs: faith, freedom and forgiveness.

Faith—having hope and courage to break out from anger and rage following injustice

I find my hope in God. It is only because of my relationship with Him and through prayer and constant communicating with Him that I found the courage to seek help to let go of the anger I felt inside. My faith in God influenced me to go to a deliverance ministry that helped me deal with the areas where I had underlying trauma. I went to a weekend retreat and experienced God's deliverance from anger and rage and now live authentically.

Freedom—being released from the chains of unforgiveness that capture us as victims

For years I felt as if there were chains on me that kept pulling me back from being who God was calling me to be. I was often timid and fearful, and I did not completely trust anyone. I felt like I was locked into victimhood. I didn't want to be a prisoner living as a victim; I knew I needed to be free and had to search for help. The chains of unforgiveness can be broken through prayer as nothing is impossible for God.

I started by asking God in many prayers to help me because I knew I couldn't free myself and was struggling. God's Word says,

"Ask, and it shall be given you (Matthew 7:7 KJV). God wants us to be free! He gave us the Holy Spirit, the Comforter, and wherever the spirit of the Lord is, there is liberty and freedom. We have the power to change things through our words.

There are a few prayers in the *Process for breaking out* on the next page; you can read them or pray aloud. Your words have the power to bring positive and negative things into your life. Many of us have been held hostage by things in our lives, but please don't let unforgiveness keep you chained as a captive or victim. Choose freedom, relieve yourself of the baggage and receive the peace that comes when you forgive.

Forgiveness—releasing resentment or vengeance consciously and deliberately

Forgiveness is a conscious and deliberate decision you make to release feelings of resentment or vengeance toward a person (or group) who has harmed you—regardless of whether they deserve or request your forgiveness.

Forgiveness does not mean forgetting, nor does it mean condoning or excusing offences. Forgiveness is not about the other person—it is about you. It is not about them making amends or confessing to their actions. It is about letting them go, releasing them to God, and marching into your freedom.

Process for breaking out

Step 1: Deciding to Forgive

Deciding to forgive is powerful and crucial to your breaking out. It is the key to opening the window you are stuck behind.

As children of God, we must forgive if we want to be forgiven. Matthew 6:14-15 NKJV says: "If you forgive those who sin against you, your heavenly Father will forgive you. But if you refuse to forgive others, your Father in heaven will not forgive your sins. Colossians 3:13 NLT states: "Make allowance for each other's faults and forgive anyone who offends you. Remember the Lord forgave you, so you must forgive others."

Forgiveness gave me freedom from the chokehold of bitterness. While I lived my life filled with unforgiveness and resentment, I felt as if I was suffocating. I frequently got headaches and felt unwell. I felt as if bitterness was sucking the life out of me. I felt as if I was dying. Being a believer in God, I knew I had to forgive, yet I wrestled with the thoughts, *It's not fair, after all the things they did to me. Why do I have to forgive them?*

Even though it was not your fault that you were abused, if you hold on to unforgiveness and never let go of the pain the person caused you, bitterness will become a yoke you wear wherever you go, whether you want to or not. It is a heavy burden! It seems so wrong that a pedophile can disrupt a child's life, leaving them permanently scarred and then just move on and flourish, free from the consequences of their actions. Nevertheless, choose to forgive for your own sake so you can be free from choking bitterness.

In this process, you might also need to forgive yourself. I chose to release myself from shame and guilt and to forgive myself for my involuntary participation in the CSA. I didn't know what was right or wrong. Later I discovered that I had been beguiled and bribed, and I refused to experience guilt or shame or feel like a fool. I had to release myself through prayers and inner healing from that shame and guilt.

We can often be distraught with ourselves and blame ourselves for not doing something or not being strong enough to stop the abuse. If you are angry with yourself for being stupid, weak or naïve, or feeling helpless like I was, be reminded it was not your fault.

Sometimes we blame our parents for not being there. That means we also have to forgive them too, even though it wasn't their fault either.

Last and definitely not least, if you blamed God or were holding a grudge against Him, just know that it wasn't God's fault. Your abuser chose to abuse you, so you need to stop being mad at God. He's been way too good to you for you to carry on toting your pains and scars.

Give it a try; it's worth a shot. Wouldn't it be great to get outside of the mental prison of *I wish I did, I shoulda, woulda, coulda done…*?

Your life and future generations depend on you and your example. When you die, wouldn't it be nice for someone to say, "She was a strong person who relied on God and refused to let past wrongs, issues or circumstances define them; she was resilient. She refused to be a victim but chose to be a victor, a champion. She chose not to be bitter or resentful. She chose to be joyful, filled with life, hope, and love. She was not selfish. She was considerate and compassionate toward others."

There is no excuse for abuse but let us think for a moment. Your abuser could also have been abused in the past, which could have been one reason they abused you. Such abuse could have caused them to think the abuse was normal. However, that never excuses their choice to abuse someone else.

I believe sin is the reason for these choices. Sin started with Adam and Eve in Genesis, hence humanity's fall from righteousness. Although that person could have just been a sick pervert, this healing journey is not about them. It is about you. It's about you being free, being "you," being "who you are destined to be." So much has been stolen from you already; why let anything else be taken from you without your consent?

Haven't you been trapped long enough? Aren't you tired of living behind the windows of a smile? Aren't you tired of putting on the façade?

Now you can stand up for yourself and say, "No, I don't want that," or "I don't like that." You can stay, "Stop!" or "Enough is enough!" It is time for you to take a proactive stand for freedom in your mind, heart, body, soul and life.

If you are ready to get out from behind the window of your smile, make that decision to forgive and don't stop there. Move on to the next part of the process, which is the prayer of forgiveness.

Step 2: Praying for Forgiveness

Let's walk through the prayer of forgiveness. Before doing that, I'd like to caution you that you might not feel like anything has changed after you say the prayer of forgiveness. However, please be encouraged and empowered in your heart that something has changed in the spiritual realm. Spoken words are powerful, either positively or negatively. That is why the Bible says: "death and life are in the power of the tongue" (Proverbs 18:21A KJV.)

When you cut off the hold of abuse by using your words, you switch off the magnet that causes you to continue attracting abusive people toward you. There are usually no immediate feelings of forgiveness, but you will feel things improve. The process of forgiveness is something we do by making the declaration out loud and meaning it because we want change in our lives. You must own your experience and make a choice, whether to persevere and walk through the process, which I'll share with you in Step 3.

Whether you pray or not is up to you. You made it this far, so why not try? Let's pray.

Heavenly Father, I come to you in the name of your son, Jesus. I come to you knowing that with you, I can do all things. Today I truly want to forgive (name of abuser). I choose to forgive (name of abuser) for abusing me, manipulating, violating my body and causing me pain. Father, I pray that you will help me release (name of abuser) as of today for violating, abusing and causing pain and trauma in my life. He/she owes me nothing, I surrender (name of abuser)'s life and my life to you. I ask that you will forgive me for condemning (name of abuser) and for holding bitterness in what was sucking the life out of me. I cast every care at your feet now. In Jesus' name, I pray amen.

Step 3: The Process of Blessing

Now that you have finished the prayer, the next thing is to walk through—or crawl through, if you can't walk—the process of blessing the person. In the process of blessing someone, you are portraying the love of God, which is supernatural. It's completely the opposite of natural love, which often comes with conditions, such as, if you're mean to me, I'll be mean to you. As believers, we are called to do unto others as we want done unto us. By going through this process, you are choosing to rely on the strength of the Holy Spirit to guide you and give you the strength and will to forgive.

The process of blessing can be a bit tricky for many. You might think, *Bless?! Are you kidding me? After everything this person did to hurt me? It hurt so bad it ruined my life; my decisions and perceptions have been altered by the trauma inflicted on me. Why should I bless that person, love them, and show them kindness? What?!*

At least, that's what I thought when I got to that point as a young adult.

A wonderful explanation came from Pastor Garfield Fray, who told me that "when you bless a person, you are asking God to give them what they need." That could be good things in their eyes—and not such good things—like health, discipline, wealth, punishment, consequence, death, etc. Each time you bless your abuser, you release yourself from being a victim, an abuse magnet, no good, worthless, not good enough, etc.

The truth is that God did not create us to be any of these things; that is not what He wants for us. Romans 12:14, 20, 21 KJV says: "bless them which persecute you: bless and curse not. 20) Therefore, if thine enemy hunger, feed him; if he thirst, give him drink: for in doing so thou shalt heap coals of fire on his head. 21) Be not overcome of evil, but overcome evil with good."

When you bless the person who has hurt you, you free yourself inside and out. So why not give it a try? Start out simply with: *"God bless (name of abuser). In Jesus' name, I pray. Amen."*

That may seem too short for a prayer meant to be a blessing, but that is okay. It really is that simple. The motive and intention behind the blessing are more important than its length, so mean what you say and say what you mean.

Ask God to make your heart and motives pure as you bless the person who abused you. Psalm 19:14 KJV says: "Let the words of my mouth, and the meditation of my heart, be acceptable in thy sight, O Lord, my strength, and my redeemer."

If you are struggling or having difficulty in this area, I suggest that you ask God to let your heart be in the right place when you are speaking or praying blessings over the person's life. In Psalm 51:10 KJV, David asked the Lord to "create in me a clean heart, O God; and renew a right spirit within me."

If our hearts are not right and we still want our abuser to die or burn, we haven't forgiven them. That's why forgiveness is the first step to moving out from behind the window of a smile.

7. I Dare You!

Behind the Windows of a Smile is a very brief yet in-depth depiction of my experience. Today, over twenty years after starting this book, I have finally gained the courage to complete it and let my courage rise above the selfishness of fear and shame so that I can be the selfless and loving woman God created me to be. I am growing bolder, stronger and I have a bright future. I couldn't always believe or express that, but God has kept me and delivered me from my past fears and low self-esteem.

I would like to dare you to do a few things. I encourage you today to break free from the bondage of being a victim—you deserve to live a blessed, happy and enjoyable life. You deserve to live in freedom. There are way too many people who have fought for you so you could be free and enjoy life in this world.

Why should your abuser live a completely victorious life, and you live a life of defeat, insecurity, fear and timidity? Why should you be the dysfunctional one?

I encourage you to live, love, dream and overcome your issues—now.

If you don't, I promise you that this problem will affect your future, your family and your generations to come. It did mine.

And it doesn't only affect you—it can and may affect anyone around you, including your spouse, your children, your parents, your friends, co-workers, or anyone else you come into contact with.

Dare to open your mouth.

Dare to talk to someone.

Dare to not allow fear rule your life.

Dare to not be angry at the world and the people you love because of your past.

Dare to seek help.

If you can relate to my story and haven't dealt with the root issue causing you pain, don't give your abuser another day for stealing another piece of your life.

As adults, we are responsible for our life choices, so we need to do something different to experience freedom and change in our lives.

Dare to love instead of fight, even when anger wants you to destroy a life. While you're trying to take a life, you are taking yours as well by choosing not to forgive. "Vengeance is mine, I will repay says the Lord" (Romans 12:9B NKJV). Maybe it felt like God wasn't there, but He was. He protected you, and He knows you're an overcomer.

I dare you to search and find out who you really are and who you are meant to be. I dare you to never forget you were spared from being destroyed, YOU ARE NOT DESTROYED! John 10:10 NKJV: "The thief does not come except to steal, and to kill, and to destroy. I (God) have come that they may have life, and that they may have it more abundantly."

I encourage you to take comfort in the fact that you are alive for a purpose and there is a reason you are here. God did not allow you to be destroyed and today is the day to break out from CSA's chains and walk out of bondage into freedom. You were born for greatness. You are fearfully and wonderfully made, and God made no mistake when He made you. He made you just right.

The diverse challenges or circumstances that you or I have faced may have blurred our perceptions but let us put aside our old perceptions and mindset and thrive on the lessons we have learned. It is not easy for anyone to change their thinking, myself included, but nothing good comes easy.

May you be empowered to take this life-altering step for yourself because YOU should matter to YOU.

Be strong, be yourself; the Holy Spirit in you is great. The Holy Bible in 1 John 4:4b KJV says: "…greater is He that is in you than he that is in the world."

Conclusion

This book was written to share my testimony and be a helping hand to someone else who needs information like this to break out from behind the window of a smile. Though this is not an in-depth study, it contains useful tools. It shares information from my experience of CSA and information about topics such as grooming, revictimization, trauma, façade smiles, coping mechanisms, triggers, communicating with family, distorted perceptions, forgiveness and blessings.

I hope these tools will enlighten you and help you see outside of the box of CSA being a taboo topic. I hope you will use the tools to help you protect your children, families and others from living behind the grim window of a smile.

Knowledge is a fantastically powerful tool, and you can use it to help yourself and others. Don't keep this book to yourself. Please share it with others to make a difference in the lives of others who may be living behind the stricken window of a smile.

Please remember that help is just a phone call away. You'll find some useful contacts in the next section, "Where to Find Help."

There are many counsellors who understand and will be willing to walk with you on your journey to healing and freedom. There are inner healing ministries, prayer partners and intercessory prayer warriors who can pray with you and help you move from behind the windows of a smile.

I made it with help and so can you!!! Choose today to walk in victory and freedom with a smile that radiates from the inside out.

Where to Find Help

Telephone

If you are in danger or believe someone is in immediate danger call 911.

- ✓ **Sexual assault Hotline**: 1-800-656-HOPE(4673) Available 24 hours a day, 7 days a week.

- ✓ **Child Help National Child Abuse Hotline**: 1-800-422-4453 Available 24 hours a day, 7 days a week.

- ✓ **Canada Suicide Prevention Service**: 1-833-456-4566

- ✓ **Distress Centres Ontario:** 416-486-2242

- ✓ **Kids Help Phone:** 1-800-668-6868

Websites

- ✓ www.crisisservicescanada.ca

- ✓ www.protectchildren.ca

- ✓ www.heretohelp.bc.ca www.thepragmaticparent.com

- ✓ https://www.aamft.org/Consumer_Updates/Childhood_Sexual_Abuse.aspx

- ✓ http://www.child-encyclopedia.com/importance-early-childhood-development/according-experts/early-brain-development-and-human

- ✓ https://raisingchildren.net.au/teens/mental-health-physical-health/sexual-assault-sexual-abuse

- ✓ https://www.thinkuknow.co.uk/parents/Concerned-about-your-child/

- ✓ https://www.protectchildren.ca/pdfs/C3P_CSAinSchoolsReport_en.pdf

- ✓ https://www.dana.org/article/wounds-that-time-wont-heal/

- ✓ https://www.inspq.qc.ca/en/sexual-assault/understanding/perpetrators

- ✓ https://www.1202.org.il/en/union/info/statistics/general-statistics

- ✓ https://www.1202.org.il/en/union/info/what-is-sexual-abuse

- ✓ https://www.mentalhelp.net/search-results/?q=sexual+abuse

- ✓ https://www.psychologytoday.com/ca/blog/fostering-freedom/202005/revictimization-how-can-keep-happening

- ✓ https://ask4ufe.com/revictimization-hidden-truth-behind-childhood-sexual-abuse/

- ✓ https://developingchild.harvard.edu/media-coverage/take-the-ace-quiz-and-learn-what-it-does-and-doesnt-mean/

- ✓ https://e2epublishing.info/blog/2014/1/20/10-confronting-child-sexual-abuse-statistics?rq=sexual%20abuse

- ✓ https://e2epublishing.info/blog/2014/5/9/protect-your-child-from-sexual-abuse?rq=protect%20your%20child%20from%20sexual%20abuse

- ✓ https://ct.counseling.org/2014/06/the-toll-of-childhood-trauma/

- ✓ https://www.thesilverlining.com/safety-tips/peer-abuse

- ✓ https://www.goodtherapy.org/learn-about-therapy/issues/sexual-abuse

For Inner Healing
- ✓ Singing Waters: 1-519-941-0929

- ✓ canadasozo.com: Susan Rashotte – susanroshotte@gmail.com

- ✓ Pastor Dwight and Laurie Richards: Dayspring Christian Church and Walking In Wholeness Ministries – info@dayspringchurch.net 905-792-1225

For Counselling, Psychologist, Psychotherapist
- ✓ Shrimattee Ault: mainoffice@alliedpsych.ca

- ✓ https://sexualassaultsupport.ca/support/

- ✓ RoxanneFrancis: hello@francispsychotherapy.com 289-275-7275
  (Instagram: @francispsychotherapy)

- ✓ Natacha Pennycooke: info@alliedpsych.ca 416-487-0791

For prayer
- ✓ info@shammahoutreach.com

- ✓ www.crossroads.ca or Crossroads Prayerline: 1-866-273-4444

- ✓ International Prayer Explosions Ministries janet@janetgordonministries.com

To contact the author in Canada
tonyakwrites@gmail.com

FreedomtoBme.com

VICTORY GOAL SETTING LOG

"Write the vision and make it plain on tablets,

that he may run who reads it" (Habakkuk 2:2 NKJV).

This is a place to start writing goals that will help you to pursue victory along your journey.

_____

_____

_____

_____

_____

_____

_____

_____

_____

References

Canadian Mental Health Association. (2013). *Childhood Sexual Abuse: A Mental Health Issue.* https://cmha.bc.ca/documents/childhood-sexual-abuse-a-mental-health-issue-2/

Darkness to Light. (2015). *Child Sexual Abuse Statistics: Risk Factors.* Darkness to Light. https://www.d2l.org/wp-content/uploads/2017/01/Statistics_4_Risk_Factors.pdf

DefendInnocence.org. (2021). *Get the Facts About Child Sexual Abuse.* Defend Innocence.org https://defendinnocence.org/child-sexual-abuse-facts/

Educate 2 Empower. (2014). *10 Confronting Child Sexual Abuse Statistics.* Educate 2 Empower Blog. https://e2epublishing.info/blog/2014/1/20/10-confronting-child-sexual-abuse-statistics?rq=child%20sexual%20abuse%20statistics

Engel, B. (2019) *Why Survivors of Child Sexual Abuse Are Often Re-victimized.* Psychology Today. https://www.psychologytoday.com/au/blog/the-compassion-chronicles/201905/why-survivors-child-sexual-abuse-are-often-re-victimized

Fadelici, K. (2020). Revictimization: *How Can This Keep Happening?: Moving from judgement to compassion.* Psychology Today. https://www.psychologytoday.com/au/blog/fostering-freedom/202005/revictimization-how-can-keep-happening

Government of South Australia. (2020*). Coping after sexual assault.* SA Health.

https://www.sahealth.sa.gov.au/wps/wcm/connect/public+content/sa+health+internet/conditions/rape+and+sexual+assault/coping+after+a+sexual+assault

Government of Western Australia, Department of Health. (2021.) *Sexual Assault.* https://healthywa.wa.gov.au/Articles/A_E/About-sexual-assault

Jaffe, A. E., DiLillo, D., Gratz, K.L., Messman-Moore, T.L. (2019). *Risk for revictimization following interpersonal and noninterpersonal trauma: Clarifying the role of posttraumatic stress symptoms and trauma-related cognitions.* Journal of Traumatic Stress, 32(1), 42-55. https://doi.org/10.1002/jts.22372

Mayo Clinic. (2020). *Anger Management: your questions answered.* Mayo Clinic Health Information: Healthy Lifestyle: Adult Health https://www.mayoclinic.org/healthy-lifestyle/adult-health/in-depth/anger-management/art-20048149

MentalHelp.net. (2021). *What is anger?* American Addiction Centers. https://www.mentalhelp.net/anger/what-is-it/

Mohammed, F. (2015). *The Repetition Compulsion: Why Rape Victims Are More Likely To Be Assaulted Again.* GirlsGlobe.org. https://www.girlsglobe.org/2015/08/04/the-repetition-compulsion-why-rape-victims-are-more-likely-to-be-assaulted-again/

Murray, L. K., Nguyen, A., & Cohen, J. A. (2014). *Child sexual abuse*. Child and adolescent psychiatric clinics of North America, *23*(2), 321–337. https://doi.org/10.1016/j.chc.2014.01.003

National Society for the Prevention of Cruelty to Children. (2021). *Grooming*. NSPCC Online. https://www.nspcc.org.uk/what-is-child-abuse/types-of-abuse/grooming/

Psychology Today. (2021a). *Sexual Abuse*. Psychology Today. https://www.psychologytoday.com/ca/basics/sexual-abuse#understanding-sexual-abuse

Psychology Today. (2021b). *Anger*. Psychology Today. https://www.mentalhelp.net/anger/what-is-it/

Saskatoon Sexual Assault & Information Centre. (2021). *Triggers: What Are They?* SSAIC.ca https://ssaic.ca/learning-resources/triggers-what-are-they

Stibich, M. (2021). *Top 10 Reasons to Smile Every Day*. VeryWellMind.com https://www.verywellmind.com/top-reasons-to-smile-every-day-2223755